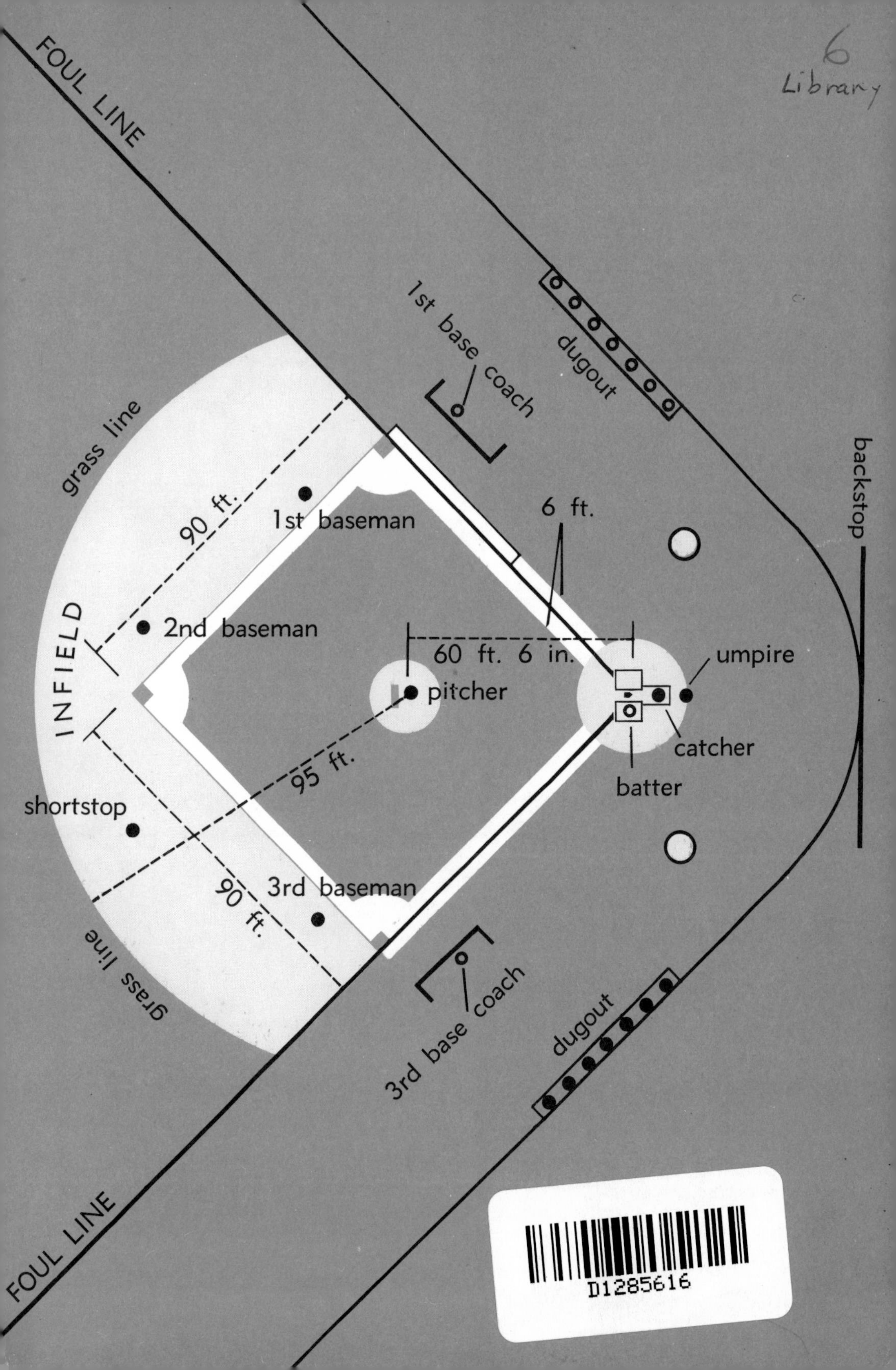

FOUL LINE

1st base coach

dugout

grass line

90 ft.

1st baseman

6 ft.

backstop

INFIELD

2nd baseman

60 ft. 6 in.

umpire

pitcher

catcher

95 ft.

batter

shortstop

3rd baseman

90 ft.

grass line

3rd base coach

dugout

FOUL LINE

ROBERTO CLEMENTE
PRIDE OF THE PIRATES

BY JERRY BRONDFIELD

ILLUSTRATED BY VICTOR MAYS

GARRARD PUBLISHING COMPANY
CHAMPAIGN, ILLINOIS

Sports Consultant:
COLONEL RED REEDER
Former Member of the West Point Coaching Staff
and Special Assistant to the West Point
Director of Athletics

Library of Congress Cataloging in Publication Data

Brondfield, Jerry, 1913-
    Roberto Clemente, pride of the Pirates.

    SUMMARY: A biography of the baseball superstar from
Puerto Rico killed in a 1972 airplane crash.

    1. Clemente, Roberto, 1934-1972—Juvenile literature.
2. Baseball—Juvenile literature. [1. Clemente,
Roberto, 1934-1972. 2. Baseball—Biography] I. Mays,
Victor, 1927-   II. Title.
GV865.C45B76   796.357′092′4 [B] [92]   75-22145
ISBN 0-8116-6675-1

Contents

1. Mission of Mercy

On the morning of December 31, 1972, a dozen people were loading boxes and crates aboard an airplane at San Juan airport in Puerto Rico. Most of the workers were men, but a few were teen-agers.

The boxes and crates contained food, medicine, clothing, shoes, and blankets.

This flight had already been delayed fifteen hours, so the workers were rushing to make up lost time. Giving orders and working harder than anyone else was Roberto Clemente, the superstar right fielder for the

Pittsburgh Pirates and Puerto Rico's most famous athlete.

It was not possible for Roberto to see where all the cargo was being placed. Crates and packages were loaded into any space the workers could find. Boxes were being piled helter-skelter one on top of the other. Nobody bothered to weigh the total amount of cargo.

A friend of Roberto Clemente's came over to him. The friend was Manny Sanguillen, the Pirates' star catcher. Like Roberto, he was a Latin American, but Manny was from Panama. He looked worried.

"Roberto," he said, "I don't like the way these things are being stowed. Nobody knows if everything will balance."

Roberto Clemente wiped his sweating brow. "We'll have to take the chance, my friend. We must get these things to Nicaragua by tonight."

6

Just a week earlier, a terrible earthquake had struck Managua, capital of the Central American country of Nicaragua. Thousands had been killed, and thousands more had been injured or were missing. Homes and stores had been destroyed. Doctors and nurses were overworked. Policemen, soldiers, and firemen were still digging for survivors.

Help was being sent from all over the world. Great Britain, Spain, Japan, Holland, and the United States were sending supplies. Puerto Rico, an American territory, decided to send its own help. The chairman of the Puerto Rican relief committee was the Pirate star, Roberto Clemente.

Roberto had taken it upon himself to go up and down streets, knocking on doors for aid. He telephoned hundreds of friends for money. He was not the kind of chairman who let others do the work.

Roberto had not expected to go to

Managua with the plane, but the president of Nicaragua had telephoned him. He told Roberto that some of the supplies sent from other nations had fallen into the hands of profiteers, who sold them instead of giving them to the needy.

Roberto was angry. "I will bring these supplies myself," he promised. "And I will see that they do not go astray."

Roberto was proud of being Puerto Rican and black. As a Puerto Rican, he had a great feeling for Latin-American neighbors in trouble. He put his whole heart into helping them.

There was another reason why Roberto wanted to go to Nicaragua. The year before, he had managed the Puerto Rican team in the world amateur baseball championship in Managua. While he was there, Roberto had gone to a hospital to visit a young boy who had lost both legs in an accident. Roberto arranged for a pair of artificial legs to be given to the boy. Roberto wanted to go back to Managua now to make sure that the boy was well. This was a good time to go —with the relief plane.

But there were people in San Juan who were afraid of the rickety old DC-7. It had been in an earlier accident, but it was the only plane available. Its engines had been repaired, and it had two new propellers. The flight had been set for early that morning, but then even more repairs were needed. The pilot, copilot, and flight engineer seemed cheerful. But Manny Sanguillen worried about the flight. There had not been time to test-fly the aircraft.

"I wish you were not going," Sanguillen told his friend. "I do not trust this plane."

Roberto laughed. "When your time comes and it is your turn to die, there is nothing you can do."

Finally the loading was completed, and Roberto went home to say good-bye to his three small sons. Roberto's wife, Vera, drove the children to her mother's house. Then Vera and Roberto went to the airport.

After his parents left, Robertito Clemente sobbed to his grandmother, "Daddy has gone to Nicaragua, but he's not coming back!"

Superfan Vera Clemente and the boys visit with Roberto before an evening game.

The grandmother calmed the little boy. "That is nonsense. He will be back in three days."

On the other side of the island, in Roberto's home town, his father, Melchor Clemente, was troubled too. That very morning he had said to his wife, Luisa, "I had a very bad dream. I dreamed I saw an airplane crash into the sea."

"It was not our Roberto's plane," his wife said. "God will not do such a thing to our son."

"But Roberto should not be making this trip on New Year's Eve," said Melchor. "He should be home with his family."

New Year's Eve is very special to Puerto Rican families. It is not only a time for joy but also for prayer.

When Vera and Roberto Clemente reached the airport late in the afternoon, Vera kissed Roberto good-bye. Then she kissed him Happy New Year. "Do not wait for us to take off," the Pirates' star told her. "We still have things to do. Go back to the children."

Later Roberto and his three crew members climbed into the old DC-7. Roberto looked around at the cargo. Everything seemed secure.

The pilot started the engines. Slowly the plane rumbled down the runway. Finally it lifted off and headed out over the Atlantic Ocean. Strong winds had whipped up high waves. The plane circled to begin its westward route to Nicaragua, 1,200 miles away.

A moment later there was an explosion in one engine. The pilot radioed the San Juan control tower. "We are turning back!"

The old DC-7 made a sharp left turn to return to the airport. Within seconds there were two more explosions. Then there was another. The DC-7 nosed over and plunged

into the huge waves of the dark Atlantic. In a moment it had sunk from sight.

The news spread rapidly. The people of Puerto Rico were shocked. Hearing the report at home, Vera Clemente cried, "It cannot be!"

Soon word of the crash was on every radio and television program in the United States. The next day was New Year's Day, and several big football bowl games were to be played. Reporters in the pressbox at the Rose Bowl game and at the Orange Bowl game found it hard to think about football. They were thinking of the great Roberto Clemente, whose plane had crashed at sea.

People everywhere hoped that he had survived. Perhaps he and the crew members had gotten into a rubber raft. Air patrols were searching the seas. Divers were attempting to find the plane beneath the surface.

Boys in Puerto Rico were heartbroken. Roberto Clemente, Puerto Rico's greatest hero, was specially loved by young boys. They knew that he had planned to build a great public park for the young people of Puerto Rico. Playing fields, equipment — everything needed for all sports —would be there. And it would be free to everyone. Much of it would be paid for by Roberto himself.

"They will find him alive," cried Luis Ortiz, a twelve-year-old fan. "A man like Roberto Clemente would get out of a crash like that. You will see!"

But after a week-long search, Luis and thousands of other Puerto Ricans had to accept the truth. The superstar of the Pittsburgh Pirates would never play again. Roberto Clemente, the greatest baseball player Puerto Rico had ever produced, was dead.

2. Black, Puerto Rican, and Proud

Baseball fans would always remember Roberto Clemente as one of the greatest players of all time. As an outfielder, he ranked with such modern heroes as Joe DiMaggio, Mickey Mantle, Ted Williams, Willie Mays, and Henry Aaron.

What made Roberto Clemente so great? He could do everything. He could hit. He could field. He could throw. He could run bases. He had a fierce determination to win, and he went all-out on every play, even if his team was behind by seven or eight runs. He did not know what it meant to give less than his very best.

"Roberto Clemente," said one baseball writer, "is the kind of player a team dreams about but rarely gets. Players like Clemente come along perhaps once or twice in a team's lifetime."

The Pittsburgh Pirates were lucky to have had him for all the eighteen years he played in the major leagues. He ranked in the top ten of all-time National Leaguers in games played, times at bat, and in hits, singles, and bases. His lifetime career batting average was a brilliant .317.

He won the National League's Golden Glove Award twelve times for his brilliant fielding. No other winner ever got as many votes for the award as he did.

Roberto was also selected for the All-Star game eleven times. He was named the National League's Most Valuable Player, and

Clemente's up! Roberto stands well back of the plate, grasps the bat firmly—and waits for the next good pitch.

he won the Outstanding Player Award in a World Series.

It is hard to judge whether Roberto was a more valuable hitter or fielder. Some days he would win the game with his bat. As a batter his eagle eyes could follow the ball's blazing path every foot of the way from the pitcher. Other days he would win it with a spectacular catch or a mighty throw.

When Roberto first started with the Pirates, he swung at many bad pitches. He knew that they were bad. "Nobody wants to hit the baseball as much as Roberto," said his first big-league manager, Fred Haney. "It is his biggest challenge. So he goes up to the plate and starts swinging."

Roberto was so eager to swing that he became famous for slashing at the first pitch, no matter where it was. Often it would be a bad one, which the umpire would have called "ball one."

"I can't stand to wait," said the young Roberto. "I must attack!" It did not take long for his manager and coaches to convince him that he should wait. If he waited for good pitches, his hitting would improve. The pitchers would have to put the ball in the strike zone. Then Roberto could attack!

Roberto attacked so well that in thirteen seasons of his career he hit over .300. In 1967 he hit an amazing .357. He set a National League record by getting ten hits in a row in two straight games, five in each game. He was only the second player in baseball history to hit safely in all the games of two seven-game World Series.

Opposing pitchers dreaded the sight of the powerful Puerto Rican coming to the plate. "It was a danger signal to me," said one veteran pitcher. "No matter how well I was pitching, Roberto Clemente could ruin me with one swing of his bat."

Roberto stood far from the plate and well back in the batter's box. His powerful hands would coil slowly around the bat handle. Then he would glare at the pitcher. He always felt it was a personal battle between him and the pitcher, and he had to win the battle.

When the ball zipped in, he would wait until the last split second. He wanted to be sure where it was going. Then he would twist into the ball, whipping the bat in a slashing swing. He often waited so long that the catcher behind the plate thought Roberto was swiping the ball right out of his glove.

But Roberto's fame as a batter was no greater than his fame as a fielder. In the outfield his acrobatics were amazing. He made clutch catches inches off the ground. He made sliding catches as he bounced on one hip. After a furious run, he often

It's up and almost away in right field as Clemente leaps into the air in pursuit of a long drive.

caught the ball in the webbing of his glove. He caught long drives while leaping up against the right-field wall. He also caught the ball by reaching into the stands, robbing batters of home runs.

Once, while running at full speed, he hit the wall. Roberto made the catch just as he crashed.

"Nobody else in the world could have held onto that ball," said another Pirate manager, Harry Walker. "Other men would have been knocked unconscious or at least dropped the ball. Clemente doesn't know the meaning of fear."

Fans said he had a rifle for a throwing arm. Often he would make a catch in deep right field and then blaze the ball in to catch a runner off first base for a double play. Nobody could make a catch, whirl around, and make the throw as fast as Roberto. Photographers often took pictures of Roberto whirling and throwing. A picture once showed Roberto suspended in the air, at least three feet off the ground. "He was in the act of releasing a lightning bolt," said one photographer.

Once Roberto Clemente did the impossible. At least no one had ever seen it done before. Playing in the outfield, he fielded a bunt! Opposing runners were on first and second, and the Pirates' shortstop was covering third. The Pirates' third baseman had crept in for the bunt that everyone knew was coming.

The batter chopped the ball to where the shortstop should have been playing. It was a long but perfect bunt. The runner from second had scored, and the runner from first was well on his way to third. Roberto came racing in from right field, the position farthest from shortstop. He scooped up the ball and threw the runner out at third.

24

"I saw it," cried a fan, "but I still don't believe it!"

Because of his strong arm, someone once asked Roberto why he did not want to pitch. "Pitchers only play every fourth day," said Roberto. "I want to play every day."

The fans often wondered how Roberto

At second base Clemente throws himself at the feet of the shortstop, breaking up a double play.

Clemente was able to play almost every day of a long season.

Unfortunately, the story of his baseball career was marked by many injuries. The tendon in his left heel constantly rubbed against the bone. The heel became inflamed and caused great pain when he ran. Floating bone chips in his elbow sometimes interfered with his throwing and his batting swing.

Roberto once had malaria, and it bothered him from time to time. He also suffered from frequent headaches and a nervous stomach.

Perhaps his biggest problem, though, came from spinal discs that had shifted and caused his back to curve slightly. Hardly a day went by when he did not feel some pain.

There were always the bumps, bruises, and muscle pulls that Roberto seemed to get more often than most players. The big reason for this was that he always gave an extra ounce of effort.

Roberto had so many injuries that the sportswriters doubted him. They thought he was a constant complainer. But Roberto's complaints were only too real. Because the writers often disbelieved him, there were bad feelings between Roberto and the press during his entire career.

Despite these problems, Roberto Clemente rose to superstardom with the Pittsburgh Pirates. It was no surprise to him or his family. Even as a small boy, Roberto Clemente knew he was going to be a great baseball player.

3. Chance at the Big Leagues

Roberto Clemente was born on August 18, 1934, in Carolina, Puerto Rico, a small village near San Juan. He was the youngest of seven children.

The Clementes were a typical black family in a typical Puerto Rican village, surrounded by sugarcane and banana plantations. Roberto's father, Melchor, was a foreman at a sugarcane plantation. He was very much respected by his neighbors. Melchor and his wife, Luisa, also ran a grocery store and meat market. English was not spoken in the Clemente home. Spanish was the only language young Roberto knew.

Although there was no poverty in the Clemente family, the children all worked, either in the fields or in the store. The parents wanted their children to know what it meant to work.

Among other things, Roberto helped load and unload trucks at the plantation. When he was nine years old, he wanted a bicycle. His father said that he would have to earn the money himself. Roberto heard of a man who was offering a penny a day to anyone who would carry a heavy milk can from a store a half-mile away. Roberto took the job, and every day he put the penny in a glass jar.

It took three years for Roberto Clemente to save enough pennies to buy a secondhand bicycle.

"My parents were wonderful," Roberto

recalled later. "I learned good habits from them and discipline, too. We didn't mind working when we understood what it would mean to us later."

But Roberto's biggest pleasure was playing ball. At first he and his friends spent hours hitting empty tin cans with sticks. By the time he was ten, he was playing softball every day on the playgrounds. Then Roberto joined a softball league. Occasionally he pitched, but more often he played shortstop.

Roberto would rather play than eat. His mother became worried.

"Roberto plays too much ball," she complained to her husband. "His health will suffer."

"Nobody's health suffers from playing games," Melchor replied. "Baseball is good for him. I'd rather have him playing ball than hanging around on the streets and getting into trouble. I think our Roberto may be a great player someday."

Nevertheless, Luisa Clemente continued to worry. One day she threw Roberto's bat into the fire. Roberto came along just in time to rescue it. Now his mother knew how much the game meant to him. She never again said anything about his playing ball.

When he was not playing, Roberto squeezed a rubber ball in his hand to strengthen the muscles in his fingers and throwing arm.

Roberto's young friends laughed at him. "Roberto must be dreaming of the big leagues," one of them jeered. Another boy frowned. "Do not laugh, *amigo*. I think he will get there."

One day that young throwing arm would be one of baseball's greatest.

When he was fourteen, Roberto began to

play baseball in addition to softball. He had no problem making the change. It was as though he had been playing with the hard baseball on a bigger diamond all his life.

During the winter he listened to the Puerto Rican winter-league games on the radio. Many major-league stars came to Puerto Rico to play in this league during the off-season. Roberto would lie in bed, pounding his fist into his tattered glove. "I will be there," he would say softly, over and over to himself. "I will play in that league someday!"

By the time Roberto entered high school, Luisa Clemente was urging him to think of going to college. He was a good student, and she wanted him to be an engineer. But Roberto's first love was sports. Not only was he the center fielder for his high-school baseball team but he was also a track star. He threw the javelin 195 feet, high jumped

6 feet, and did 45 feet in the triple jump.
His javelin and triple-jump marks were
Puerto Rican records. Everyone expected
that he would aim for the 1956 Olympics in
Australia. But it was baseball that won out.

Roberto Marin, who had coached Roberto
as a softball player, got in touch with a
man named Pedro Zorilla. Zorilla was the
owner of the Santurce team, a Puerto
Rican team in the winter league. "You

must take a good look at this boy," Marin urged Zorilla. "I think you will agree that he could become a star."

Zorilla was not interested. Everyone gave him names of players who might become stars. Then one day he wandered over to a high-school game near San Juan. Zorilla's eyes widened as he watched a graceful, seventeen-year-old center fielder. The boy hit a 400-foot triple and two line-drive doubles. He also nailed a runner at third with a bullet throw from deep center.

"Who is he?" Zorilla asked a youth next to him.

"Oh, that's Roberto Clemente," the boy told Zorilla.

Pedro Zorilla wasted no time in offering Roberto a bonus of $300 if he would play with the Santurce team. Roberto's parents did not think the offer was good enough, so Zorilla raised the bonus to $500. He also promised the young player $60 a month and a free glove.

Roberto Clemente was on his way to a professional baseball career. He was supposed to join the Santurce team the following winter. Meanwhile, major-league scouts had heard of him. That summer the Dodgers, who were still in Brooklyn, New York, held a tryout camp in San Juan. One of the 100 players invited was Roberto Clemente. Thousands of Puerto Rican youths dreamed of being invited to a tryout. There major-league clubs could watch them play— and maybe offer them contracts.

The Dodgers' camp director was Al Campanis, a big-league scout for over 30 years. He was amazed by Roberto's hitting, fielding, throwing, and running. That night Campanis hurried to see Melchor Clemente. He said that he wanted to sign Roberto for the Dodgers' minor-league farm system.

Melchor Clemente refused to sign. "I want Roberto to finish high school first. Come back next year."

That season Roberto played right field in the Puerto Rican winter league. And beside him in center field was the New York Giants' great Willie Mays!

Roberto's friends thought Roberto would be nervous playing beside such a star. "Why should I be nervous?" Roberto said calmly. "He will do what he has to do, and I will do what I must do."

"Ah, and you can learn from him!" they said.

"Yes, perhaps I can," said Roberto. Then he thought for a moment. "Who knows — maybe Willie Mays will like something *I* do — and learn from me!"

The following spring nearly a dozen big-league scouts came to town. They all hoped to sign Roberto. The Dodgers got to him first and offered him a $10,000 bonus to sign. It was the largest bonus ever offered a Latin American. That included offers that had been made earlier to such superstars as Felipe Alou and Juan Marichal.

Roberto said he would accept. But a few hours later, a man from the Milwaukee Braves told Roberto he would give him a bonus of $30,000!

Melchor and Luisa Clemente took their son aside. "Yes, this is much more than the man from the Dodgers said he would give you," said Melchor. "A fortune! But you have given your word to the Dodgers. Your word is worth more than money."

So Roberto Clemente accepted the offer of the Brooklyn Dodgers, and on February 19, 1954, the contract was signed. Roberto was sure he would like the Dodgers. They had been the first club to take a black man onto a major-league team. That black man, Jackie Robinson, was one of Roberto's heroes.

Young Roberto wondered where he would start his professional career. As a nineteen-year-old, he could expect to begin playing in one of the lowest minor leagues, perhaps Class C or Class D. These were small-town leagues in states such as South Dakota, North Carolina, and Iowa.

But the Dodgers thought Roberto's talent held more promise than that. During the 1954 season, his first in organized baseball, they sent him to join Montreal of the Triple-A International League. This was the top of the minor leagues. Young Roberto was surprised. But if the Dodgers had confidence in him, he would not let them down.

Nor would he let his parents or his six brothers and sister down. "This is my chance," he said quietly as he left home. "I will make the most of it."

40

4. Injuries and Insults

Although Roberto Clemente had great confidence in himself, things were not easy for him when he joined Montreal in 1954. He reported with a bad back, an injury that would bother him throughout his career.

Roberto had always used a heavy bat until his first season with Santurce. At that time hitters were beginning to use lighter ones. They found that the faster swing of a light bat provided more distance. The first time that Roberto tried the lighter bat, he whipped it around so fast that he injured his spine.

But he was determined that his back would not stop him from getting a good start in Montreal. Whenever he felt the pain, he gritted his teeth and refused to think about it.

Meanwhile, Roberto was feeling another kind of pain—the pain of homesickness. He had never been away from home before, and he missed his family and friends.

Roberto was even more lonely because of a language problem. He had studied English in high school but had never spoken it outside the classroom. Now, for the first time, he had to speak English with strangers. To make matters worse, many people in Montreal spoke only French, the main language of the province of Quebec.

Roberto found it difficult to talk to his teammates. It would have been even harder for him if it had not been for Sandy Amaros and Chico Fernandez, two other

Latin-American ballplayers. They not only spoke Spanish but could also speak English quite well.

Pitcher Joe Black, an American black, also spoke some Spanish. But if one of these three was not around, young Roberto had difficulty understanding some of the things his teammates said.

As Roberto began to learn more English, he became less homesick and began to enjoy Montreal.

He and Fernandez, who was also black, lived with a white family in a French neighborhood. For the first time in his life, Roberto began to understand the problems that can come between people whose skins are of a different color.

The two young black men were treated as equals by the white family with whom they lived. But when the Montreal team went South, it was a different story.

In Richmond, Virginia, Roberto and Chico Fernandez could not stay in the same hotel with whites or eat in the same restaurant. They had to stay in a hotel for blacks.

Often white players on rival teams hurled insults at Roberto. Some of his teammates did not treat him as an equal. Roberto found this the hardest thing to understand.

"Someday," said Roberto to Joe Black, "I will make them respect me as a great baseball player—who just happens to be black."

Roberto had a problem proving himself as a baseball player, for he did not play regularly. He knew he was the best outfielder on the Montreal club, but he played less than half the season and batted only 148 times. A regular player bats about 450 times a year.

One day Roberto hit three triples in one game. The next day the manager benched him. "I do not understand this," Roberto moaned to a teammate. He complained to his manager and to the sportswriters. Minor leaguers usually kept quiet, but not Roberto Clemente. He had too much pride and confidence in himself to remain silent.

Roberto's teammates knew that he was their best outfielder. But they also knew that the parent club, the Brooklyn Dodgers, was trying to hide Roberto. The Dodgers had many stars, and they did not need Roberto yet.

At that time, a rookie who received at least $4,000 for signing had to play a whole season with a minor-league team. At the end of the season, he had to be brought up to the major-league team that had signed him or else offered for sale to other clubs.

If Roberto was on the bench a good part of the season, other clubs would probably not want him. Then the Dodgers could keep him in Montreal another year.

5. Rookie Star of the Pirates

One day in the summer of 1954, Branch
Rickey, president of the Pittsburgh Pirates,
sent a Pirate pitching coach to Richmond,
Virginia. He wanted to check on Montreal
pitcher Joe Black. Rickey thought he might
want to buy Black from the Dodgers.

The coach, Clyde Sukeforth, was a veteran
judge of talent. He watched Black in action,
but it was a young, unknown outfielder who
caught his eye. He decided to stay a few
extra days to watch him. In his report to
Rickey, Sukeforth raved about twenty-year-
old Clemente's slashing line drives.

"He could also catch a fly ball in his hip pocket if he had to," Sukeforth added. "And he has an arm that could throw a baseball through a concrete wall!"

Sukeforth had never been so enthusiastic about a player before. Rickey trusted his judgment. But Rickey did not show his hand until the end of the season. In November 1954, the major leagues held their annual draft of minor leaguers. Having finished in last place that year, the Pirates got first choice of all the young players available. Since the Brooklyn Dodgers did not yet need Clemente in the major league, they had to offer him for sale.

Much to the Dodgers' surprise and disappointment, the Pittsburgh Pirates made Roberto Clemente their first draft choice. Sportswriters on the Pittsburgh papers knew little about the young Puerto Rican. But one of them got a tip from a Pirate scout.

Next day the reporter wrote that perhaps the Pirates had come up with a "sleeper."

The first thing Roberto said was, "I don't even know where Pittsburgh is."

In Puerto Rico Melchor Clemente smiled. "Pittsburgh will surely know where Roberto Clemente is—soon!"

The Pirates had finished last in the National League in 1952, 1953, and 1954. In 1954 they were last in team batting and pitching. They won only 53 games and lost 101. The club hit only .248 and scored 100 fewer runs than any other club in the league.

This was the team Roberto Clemente joined as a twenty-year-old rookie. He went to the Pirates' spring training camp in Fort Myers, Florida, in February 1955. Unfortunately, he was not in the best of shape. During the winter he had suffered another back injury in an auto accident.

Roberto was very unhappy about the racial segregation practiced in Florida. Once again he was forced to live and eat only with blacks. Once again his ears burned when fans hurled racial insults at him. The stands at the exhibition games were much closer to the field than those in major-league parks. Roberto could actually pick out the fans who shouted insults at him. There were times when he could hardly keep from jumping into the stands to get at those people. But he remembered how his hero, Jackie Robinson, had stood up to this problem, and Roberto controlled himself.

One thing did help him to feel at home. Outfielder Felipe Montemayor, a Mexican, and outfielder Roman Mejias, a Cuban, both spoke Spanish. So did pitcher-outfielder Dick Hall.

In spring training in Florida, for the first time in his career as an athlete, Roberto

Playing in the major league didn't guarantee success! Rookie Roberto Clemente is tagged out here in a close play at home plate.

Clemente felt pressure. Now he was in the big leagues. This was the chance he had dreamed of. If he failed, he would go back to the minors — or back to Puerto Rico.

Fred Haney, the manager of the Pirates, watched the young rookie closely. So did the veteran players. They wondered if the rookie was good enough to take a job away from one of them.

What they saw was a fierce young man who hustled every second.

"That kid thinks this is a matter of life or death!" said one veteran.

A baseball writer nodded. "Maybe that's what this ball club needs!"

The Pirates played well in spring training. They beat the American League Baltimore Orioles nine times in fourteen games. Only the Milwaukee Braves had a better record at the end of the spring exhibition season.

When the team went north to Pittsburgh, young Roberto boarded in the home of Mr. and Mrs. Stanley Garland. Mr. Garland was a postal worker who loved baseball. The Garlands were like a second mother and father to Roberto.

When the regular season began, Roberto needed their comfort and sympathy because he did not make the starting lineup. He was crushed and discouraged. He did not play in the first three games.

"Be patient, now," said Stanley Garland. "They'll have to give you your chance. And when you get it—boom!"

Stanley Garland was right. On April 17, 1955, Roberto Clemente started against the Dodgers in a doubleheader. The Pirates lost both games, but Roberto got a hit the first time he was up and scored on Frank Thomas's triple. In the second game he got a single and a double.

The next day against the Giants, Roberto smashed a homer inside the ball park. This proved his speed on the bases. He also showed his great arm when he grabbed a line drive and threw it to first base for a double play.

He was now a regular in the lineup. But as time went by, his coaches began to worry about a bad habit he had developed. He bobbed his head and took his eye off the ball as he swung. Opposing pitchers took advantage of Roberto and fooled him with change-of-pace delivery. As a result, Roberto swung at too many bad pitches.

Roberto was discouraged, but he worked on this problem every day in batting practice. Finally, through much effort and determination, he stopped bobbing his head.

Roberto's fielding had no flaws. Against Milwaukee he leaped for a one-handed catch of a ball heading for the stands. Two men were on base, and a homer would have beaten the Pirates, 5-4. But Roberto's leap saved the game. A few days later he raced to grab a fly and made a double play on a runner trying to score. It took a perfect throw to do it.

During that 1955 season, Roberto's back problem and a sprained ankle benched him off and on. Once, after having been out several days, he came back into the lineup and got five straight hits in one game — two singles and three doubles.

The Pirates finished in last place again, but they were a more spirited team. And fans were saying that in a couple of years young Roberto Clemente would lead them to the top. In his first season he had batted .255 in 124 games. He had hit 23 doubles, 11 triples, and 5 homers.

Clearly, he was one of the top rookies the 1955 season had produced.

6. "Get Out of My Way!"

In Roberto's second year with the Pirates, the team had a new manager, Bobby Bragan. The Pirates also got a new outfielder, Bill Virdon, and a new second baseman, Bill Mazeroski. Pittsburgh would be a stronger club if the players could raise their batting averages.

Roberto led the way. By early June his average was up to .348, fourth best in the National League. The Pittsburgh Pirates at one stretch won fifteen and lost twelve. This was the best showing of a Pirate team in a half-dozen years.

56

Then the team slipped. Young Roberto felt anger inside him. Why wouldn't the players fight as he did? His anger affected his batting. He began swinging wildly at everything the pitchers threw.

Once again Roberto had to learn that concentration is an important part of baseball.

"Stop trying to hit every pitch out of the park!" said batting coach, Dick Sisler. "You have to get a grip on your feelings."

Roberto controlled his temper. He began to meet the ball where it was pitched. He concentrated on hitting it between the fielders, for singles and doubles. Opposing pitchers in the league soon got the news.

"Roberto Clemente is hitting line drives that whistle and can't be stopped!" was the warning.

Against Cincinnati he hit a three-run homer to win the game. A few days later

he drove in four runs with a homer, a triple, and a sacrifice fly. The next day Roberto made even bigger news. He disregarded a coach's signal.

In the bottom of the ninth inning, the Pirates trailed the Cubs, 8-5. Then the Pirates filled the bases. Roberto came up and slammed the ball to deep center. Three runs scored, tying the game. As Roberto raced toward third, Manager Bragan, who was coaching there, gave him the stop sign.

Roberto disregarded it. He sped around third and slid home for an inside-the-park homer that won the game.

Manager Bragan shrugged wisely and agreed not to fine Roberto for disobeying his signal. Roberto grinned as he talked to reporters. "Sure, I saw Bragan's signal and heard him yell for me to stop. But I wanted to score. I just yelled back, 'Get out of my way!' and kept going."

Pirate fans were joyous. Here was a ballplayer to excite them. Roberto finished the season with a .311 batting average. This was sensational for a second-year player. He also was credited with 20 assists from the outfield, throwing out runners. His favorite stunt was to pick off a runner who was making too wide a turn at first base. Roberto would throw him out before he got back to the bag. Fans roared whenever Roberto's rifle arm did this trick.

The Pirates climbed out of the league cellar to finish in seventh place. They won a lot of games against the league's top teams.

"Watch this club," the fans began saying. "And watch that Roberto Clemente! The Pirates finally have a superstar in the making."

To reward their new spark plug, the Pirates gave Roberto a big pay raise for

1957. The first thing he did with his money was to buy a new home for his parents in Puerto Rico.

Things did not go well either for Roberto or for the Pirates during the 1957 season. Manager Bragan was replaced by Danny Murtaugh in mid-season, but the team still finished in seventh place.

Roberto's back bothered him so much that he often wore a brace when he played. He played in only 111 games, and his batting average dropped to .253.

The team doctor thought that Roberto's backache might be caused by infected tonsils. "Nothing's wrong with my tonsils," Roberto said. But he had them removed anyway. "It's my back that hurts," he insisted.

Some sportswriters reported that Roberto was a complainer. This was not fair to Roberto, for he was often in pain. But he was determined that the 1958 season would find him once again an exciting young player—the joy of the Pirate fans.

That autumn and winter Roberto did not play in the winter league in Puerto Rico. Roberto had to put in his military service. He joined the marines' reserve program and was sent to the marine base at Parris Island, South Carolina. He was there for almost six months.

He did not ask for, nor did he get, special favors. He did all the heavy work and tough drills that the other young marines did. Someone once asked why he did not try to get assigned as a clerk or some other such job.

"I came here to learn to be a marine!" Roberto glared. "And I want to do it the same way these other guys are doing it— by proving I'm as tough as anyone else!"

When he got out, just in time to join

**Clemente makes an acrobatic back-handed
catch in right-center field.**

the Pirates early in the 1958 season, his back felt better. In the opener against Milwaukee, he got two singles and a double. "Roberto is back!" his fans chanted gleefully.

They were right. His batting average climbed to .289. He became one of the team's leaders. With Roberto showing the way, the Pirates battled their way toward the top and finished second in their league.

Pittsburgh came close to winning the pennant that year. The team finished with an 84-65 record. Everyone agreed that Roberto Clemente was now the best right fielder in the National League.

The Pirates had not won a pennant in more than 30 years, and their fans were impatient. Perhaps 1959 would be the year. But early in the season Clemente was hit on the elbow by a pitch and was out of action for almost two months. The arm still hurt him when he returned to the lineup, and often he could not play. By now the sportswriters simply couldn't believe that one player could have so many injuries.

Manager Danny Murtaugh accused Roberto of slacking off. He told Roberto that if he could not help the team, then he should take off his uniform. But Roberto had too much pride to quit, and he refused. The Pittsburgh sportswriters appeared to be on the manager's side. "What about it, Roberto?" one of them asked him at the end of the season. "When are the Pirates going to win the pennant?"

It seemed to Roberto that the writers were putting the entire responsibility on him.

"Next year!" Roberto blazed at the reporter. "Write that down! Next year! And tell the fans that Roberto Clemente guarantees it!"

7. The Most Valuable Player

That winter Roberto Clemente went back to Puerto Rico and played again for the Santurce team. But it was a different Roberto Clemente. He was worried because sportswriters didn't like him. They were writing unkind things about him. They said that he was faking his injuries, and they called him the "Puerto Rican Hot Dog." It was their way of saying that he was a show-off—a player who was looking for attention and publicity. This hurt Roberto deeply, and he brooded all through the winter months.

When Roberto was not playing with the Santurce team, he spent many hours by himself. He made lamps, beautiful wood carvings, and pottery. He had real artistic talent and enjoyed the work, but his thoughts were bitter. His main goal was to be recognized as a great baseball player. But people who did not understand him were not ready to agree that he was great.

He was determined that the next season would make them change their minds.

Roberto's determination paid off. In 1960 the Pittsburgh Pirates were the most exciting team in baseball. More than 20 times, they won victories in the ninth inning. Twelve times they won after two men were out in the ninth! Their stars were Don Hoak at third base, Dick Groat at shortstop, and Roberto Clemente. Roberto Clemente was special, and the fans loved him. Every time he came up to bat, they screamed,

In an unusual attempt to protect a runner stealing second base, Roberto throws his bat at a ball—and hits it!

"Arriba!"—the Spanish word that is translated roughly, "Hit it up!"

Roberto's bat slammed out hit after hit. Nineteen times he threw out base runners. His arm had become the most feared in baseball. Once, Willie Mays of the Giants smashed a drive down the right-field line. Roberto raced over and made the catch. His speed carried him full tilt into a concrete wall. Blood streamed down his face, but he held onto the ball. Roberto spent the next five days in a hospital.

The Pirates did not play as well while Roberto was out of the lineup. Shortly after he returned, he made more sensational catches and hit home runs on three straight days. For the rest of the season, the Pirates were never in danger of losing their league lead.

In late September the St. Louis Cardinals, the only club with a chance to catch the

Pirates, lost a game with Chicago. The
Cardinals were now out of the running. The
score was posted on the board during a
Pittsburgh-Milwaukee game, and the Pirates
went wild. Roberto was on second base
after hitting a double. When the next batter hit a single, Roberto raced to third. Ig-
noring the coach's stop sign, he stormed
around third to score with a long slide. His
manager forgave him when Roberto said, "I
did not stop at third because I wanted to

70

The 1960 World Series, with Clemente at bat.

get to the bench and talk about the pennant!"

It was the first Pirates pennant in 33 years. Then the Pirates went on to beat the New York Yankees in the World Series in seven games. Although it was a home run by Bill Mazeroski that won the final game, Roberto's fielding and hitting were very important in the Series. Roberto got nine hits. He also hit safely in all seven games — a very rare feat.

But Roberto was disappointed when his teammate, Dick Groat, was chosen as the National League's Most Valuable Player by sportswriters around the nation. Roberto felt that some of the sportswriters did not like him and had kept him from winning the award. He could not help feeling bitter and angry.

Roberto was named to the National League All-Star game that season. But it was the MVP prize he had wanted more than anything. He wondered how long he would have to wait to get it.

In 1961 Roberto was a home-run threat with 23 homers. During a batting spree in August, he got 26 hits in 36 times at bat. Roberto also put in a great performance in the 1961 All-Star game. He got a triple his first time at bat. The next time up, his

Roberto Clemente, Willie Mays, and Hank Aaron, heroes of the 1960 All-Star game.

400-foot drive was just barely caught by Mickey Mantle. In extra innings it was Roberto Clemente who drove in the winning run with a single. He was so proud of his performance that he took off his 1960 World Series ring and began wearing only his 1961 All-Star ring.

The Pirates did not win the pennant that year. But Roberto led the league in hitting

73

with a sizzling .351. It was one of the highest averages in many years, and it included 201 hits. This was another rare feat for a hitter. The magic figure for hits is 200, and not many stars—even the greatest—reach it.

But again the MVP Award was not given to him. By now he was sure that the sportswriters were the reason.

In the next few years, Roberto was truly one of baseball's superstars. Eight years in a row, he hit over .300. Four times he won the National League batting crown. In 1967 he hit an amazing .357. But he could not find peace with the press or with his manager, Danny Murtaugh. In 1962, when he hit .312, a sportswriter called it "a disappointing season." Teammate Dick Groat hit .294, and the same writer said that Groat had "a fine year."

"I do not understand it," Roberto exploded to reporters. "You say I am not a team player, that I do not give my best. But I have won four batting titles. I kill myself in the outfield. I try to catch any ball in the park. I throw my arm out for the Pirates, and I play when I hurt!"

It always made Roberto angry that the writers criticized him. It bothered him that they seemed to accept Mickey Mantle's knee trouble or hip injury. But they didn't understand the bone chips in Roberto's elbow or the fact that his spine was curved. "Mickey Mantle is like a god," he once said. "But if a black or a Latin American is hurting, they say he is imagining things."

People who knew Clemente well always respected his loyalty to his teammates. Once, second baseman Bill Mazeroski was being honored before a game. Roberto, leaving the clubhouse to watch the ceremonies, suddenly stopped. He had noticed three of the Pirates sitting around playing cards. Roberto

Roberto was famous for his acrobatics in the outfield. No ball was too high or too low to escape his glove!

became angry. "They are honoring a great player and teammate out there on the field," he snapped, his eyes blazing. "I will give you three minutes to get outside to see it, or you will have to fight me!"

Despite Roberto's problems with the press, baseball fans remained loyal. They often argued over who was the better fielder— Willie Mays or Roberto Clemente. "How many times has Willie Mays been willing to crash into a wall?" demanded Roberto's supporters. "And Willie does not have Roberto's deadly arm in doubling runners off first!" they added.

Year after year Roberto was named to the National League All-Star team. Year after year he received the Golden Glove Award for his fielding.

"If only he could stay healthy," another fan moaned, "Roberto would be the greatest outfielder in the history of baseball."

But injuries continued to bother him. When the bone chips in his elbow hurt, he told Manager Murtaugh he could not play. Murtaugh said he must play or he would fine him.

Roberto did not care about a $100 fine. He was now a superstar earning $80,000 a season. But he had great pride in himself. He did not like to be accused of faking, so he played. Once, he got spiked in the ankle and went back to play after it was stitched up. When he could not run well enough to pick off line drives, he was accused of faking.

But Roberto no longer had to face his accusers alone. One day in San Juan, he went to a drugstore for some medicine. He was introduced to another customer, who had just come in. She was a tall, beautiful girl named Vera Christina Zabala. For Roberto, it was love at first sight.

They were married on November 14, 1964, in the church in which Roberto had been baptized. Fifteen hundred people came to the reception.

Roberto's life changed. Now he spent more time with friends and began to appear at civic affairs. He visited sick children in hospitals. Everyone predicted that Roberto would have a great season in 1965.

But he seemed to have been jinxed again. That winter he was seriously injured in a lawn-mower accident and had to have an operation on his leg. A few weeks later he had another attack of malaria.

The injury and the malaria cost Roberto and the Pirates several games early in the season. But then he came back stronger than ever. Because of his batting and his leadership, the Pirates came close to winning the pennant. Roberto, however, won the league batting crown with a .329

It's a hit—and Roberto is on his way to first base!

average. More important, he was also getting along well with the Pirates' new manager, Harry Walker.

Walker believed Roberto whenever he said
that his arm or back hurt. "I will leave it
up to you whether or not you should play,"
said Walker. "I trust you."

Roberto was so pleased that in 1966 he
had his greatest year and was recognized as
the team leader. In one period of less than
two weeks, he hit six homers. Two of them
cleared an exit gate in right-center field,
436 feet from home plate. Nobody in the
history of Forbes Field remembered anyone
hitting two home runs over that gate. They
must have sailed more than 500 feet.

It was a spectacular season for many
reasons. Roberto hit a sparkling .317 and
hammered in 29 homers, his all-time-high
home-run figure. He batted in 119 runs and
scored 105. One hundred is considered super

in each department. He hit 31 doubles, fifth best in the league, and 11 triples, third best. He hit for 342 total bases, second only to Felipe Alou's 355. And it was the seventh straight year that he batted .300 or over.

It was truly a great year. But would it bring Roberto Clemente the award that he wanted most?

The battle for the league's Most Valuable Player in 1966 had narrowed to two men. One was Sandy Koufax, the great pitcher for the Los Angeles Dodgers. The other was Roberto Clemente.

When the ballots were being sent in at the end of the season, Roberto was tense. He honestly felt that no player had done more for his team than he had. But he worried about his old reputation for complaining about his injuries. Perhaps now the writers had realized how great he was!

Then came the announcement. And the

winner, the National League's Most Valuable Player: ROBERTO CLEMENTE!

In Puerto Rico the news brought people, cheering, into the streets. Boys on the playgrounds tossed their battered gloves into the air. The mayors of San Juan and other large cities praised Roberto. He was the first Latin-American baseball player ever to be named Most Valuable Player. The Puerto Ricans felt as though they had their own Babe Ruth.

For Roberto Clemente, the honor meant that his chief goal had been won. He knew he was great. Now the whole baseball world thought so too. It was the most dramatic moment of his life—so far.

8. A Place in the Hall of Fame

With his usual luck, Roberto Clemente had a bad fall at his cliffside home in the winter of 1968. When he fell, he just missed tumbling over a 75-foot cliff. He badly injured his shoulder, which hurt all the next year.

One night in May of 1969, his shoulder throbbed after a game in San Diego. He decided to take his mind off the pain by going for a walk. Leaving his motel room, he went down the road to get some chicken at a take-out shop.

As he was returning to his motel, a car pulled up beside him on the dark road.

Four men were in it, and one of them pointed a gun at Roberto. They made him get in and drove to a lonely spot in the California countryside.

There they made him remove his clothes. They took his wallet, his All-Star ring, and about $250 in cash.

Roberto was sure they were going to shoot him. He told the men that he was a big-league baseball player, but they just laughed.

The man who was holding the gun put it to Roberto's head. Roberto thought he was about to die. He thought of his wife, Vera, and his sons back in Puerto Rico and said a silent prayer.

Then Roberto heard one of the four gunmen speak in Spanish. Quickly Roberto spoke to him in Spanish. "You can take my money," he said. "But do not kill for money."

They looked at him silently. "I really am a baseball player," Roberto went on. Then he told a lie. "I play for the San Diego Padres." He did not want them to know that he was Roberto Clemente of the Pirates. They might decide to hold him for ransom. Or they might become frightened because they had kidnapped someone so famous, and kill him to keep him quiet.

Suddenly they told Roberto he could go. The men drove him near his motel and let him out.

As Roberto started toward his motel, the car turned around and roared back. "This time they will kill me," Roberto thought. But one of the men leaned out and tossed a cardboard box to him. "You forgot your fried chicken," the man said.

This experience left Roberto shaken for a while. But he snapped out of it and hit .345 for the season. His average soared to

.352 in 1970. There was no question now; he was a superstar. In 1971 he led the Pirates to another World Series triumph. That year he did what he had done ten years earlier. Against the Baltimore Orioles, he hit safely in all seven World Series games. The Pirates won the deciding game, 2-1, on Roberto's home run.

Then more drama came into Roberto Clemente's life. As the 1972 season started, Roberto was only 118 hits away from the magic goal of 3,000 career hits. Ten men in baseball history had already made it: Cap Anson, Nap Lajoie, Honus Wagner, Tris Speaker, Ty Cobb, Paul Waner, Eddie Collins, Stan Musial, Willie Mays, and Hank Aaron.

Could Roberto do it? The tendons in his heels pained him in June. In July he got the flu. In August he had a stomach virus. But he kept swinging away.

Roberto Clemente, Most Valuable Player of
the 1971 World Series. His record in the
seven-game contest: 12 hits, 2 doubles, 1
triple, and 2 homers.

He had missed more than 50 games that season because of injury or illness. In August a sportswriter said to him, "It looks like time is running out on you, Roberto."

"We shall see," said Roberto grimly. He went into the last 26 games needing 25 hits to reach the magic milestone. But now the tendons in his heels were bothering him again. "I don't want to play when I can't do my best," he said.

So he missed some more games. On the last road trip of the season, he got hit number 2,999 off the Phillies' Steve Carlton. Just two more games were left, both at home.

In the first of the two games, he faced the New York Mets' great Tom Seaver. The Pittsburgh Pirates' new ball park, Three Rivers Stadium, was full of excited fans.

In the first inning Roberto hit a bouncer off Seaver's glove. The Mets' second baseman, Ken Boswell, came in to field it. It skipped off his glove, and Roberto was at first.

At first a huge *H*, for "hit," lit up on the scoreboard. The crowd went wild. But the official scorer in the pressbox had called an error. The *H* on the scoreboard was changed to an *E* for "error." The crowd booed, but the *E* stood. His last time at bat, Roberto sent a scorching liner to the right-field corner, which Rusty Staub grabbed for the out. Normally, Staub did not play that close to the line for Roberto. He said later that he had wandered over without realizing it. Seaver held Roberto in check the rest of the game.

After the game reporters asked Roberto what he thought of the decision on the ground ball in the first inning.

"I would not have wanted the official scorer to call it a hit if he wasn't sure of

Arriba! Roberto hits Number 3,000 and
becomes the eleventh player in baseball
history to reach the magic number.

it," said Roberto. "I don't want my 3,000th hit to be a cheap one or a gift, to leave doubt in the fans' minds."

So now there was only one day left in the 1972 season. The next afternoon the Pirates faced the Mets' Jon Matlack. For Roberto, that meant more drama.

Matlack had not allowed Roberto a hit in the several games he had pitched against him that year. Would the jinx hold? Would Roberto have to wait for the 1973 season to get his 3,000th hit? What if Roberto's injuries forced him to retire before the season started? He would have finished his career with 2,999 hits. So near, yet so far.

A few minutes after three o'clock the next day, the suspense was ended. Roberto saw Matlack's curve breaking toward the plate. He swung and lashed the ball to deep left-center field for a double. Standing on second base, Roberto felt his heart pounding as he tipped his cap to the roaring fans. He had his 3,000th hit. The ball was thrown in to him as a souvenir. He said that he would dedicate it to the fans of Pittsburgh and Puerto Rico and to Roberto Marin, the man who had given him his first chance in baseball.

No one could guess at that time how fortunate Roberto had been in his last game of the season. There would never be another season for Roberto Clemente. There would never be hit number 3,001.

Roberto Clemente was killed in the plane that crashed on the mercy flight to Nicaragua the winter after his 3,000th hit.

Church bells tolled in Puerto Rico and in every Puerto Rican community in the United States. In Pittsburgh a huge advertising sign, high on a hill, turned off its usual message for a new one. In electric letters that were visible for many miles, it said: *"ADIOS AMIGO ROBERTO."* "Goodbye friend Roberto."

In Puerto Rico it was announced that Roberto's fondest dream would become a reality. He had always wanted to build a *Ciudad Deportiva*—a City of Sport—in San Juan for the young people. Facilities for all kinds of sports would be built there: baseball, basketball, boxing, swimming, track and field, and tennis. Professional instructors would be hired for every sport. And it would be free for the boys and girls of Puerto Rico. It would be the biggest, most complete public sports park in the world.

When Roberto died, money came in from everywhere to build the park. Land was set aside. The Puerto Rican government promised that yearly funds would be made available to operate it.

Only three months after Roberto's death,

the Baseball Writers Association of America held a meeting. This is the group that elects players to the Baseball Hall of Fame. The rule is that a player must be out of baseball five years before he is eligible for election.

They changed the rule for Roberto Clemente and held a special election. On March 20, 1973, Roberto Clemente was voted into the Baseball Hall of Fame —beside Babe Ruth, Lou Gehrig, Ty Cobb, Joe DiMaggio, and other superstars of baseball. He was the first Latin-American player to make it.

Roberto Clemente would have liked that. There no longer was any doubt that he was one of the greatest and bravest players in baseball history.